Guitar Fitness

AN EXERCISING HANDBOOK

BY JOSQUIN DES PRES

T0053081

Contents

ISBN 978-0-7935-1697-1

HAL•LEONARD®
CORPORATION

7777 W. BLUEMOUND RD. P.O. BOX 13819 MILWAUKEE, WI 53213

The purpose of this book is to provide the aspiring guitar player with a wide variety of finger exercises indispensable to anyone wanting to develop the technique necessary to succeed in today's music scene. It can also play a very important role in a player's daily practicing program.

These exercises are designed to help **increase your speed, improve your dexterity, develop accuracy** and **promote finger independence** Even though all the tablatures and finger combinations apply to the left hand, they will also work your right hand as some of them require swift and precise right hand moves. The numbers on the tablature indicate both frets and fingers:

Number 1 indicates the index finger as well as fret 1.
Number 2 indicates the middle finger as well as fret 2.
Number 3 indicates the ring finger as well as fret 3.
Number 4 indicates the little finger as well as fret 4.

Practice daily, playing each exercise **for at least 15 minutes** before moving on to the next one. Play each exercise up and down, then move up chromatically in half steps (a half step equals one fret). Starting at fret 1 up to the 12th fret and back down.

Always use a metronome, playing eighth notes (two notes per metronome click). Start at the **slowest indicated speed, concentrate on your sound,** then gradually speed up. When crossing over strings, be as precise as possible by watching alternately your left and right hand.

Part A

Exercises with all 4 fingers moving across the fingerboard

♩ = 60/180

UP

4

DOWN

UP

5

DOWN

UP

6

DOWN

♩ = 60/180

UP

7

DOWN

UP

8

DOWN

UP

9

DOWN

♩ = 60/180

UP

10

DOWN

UP

11

DOWN

UP

12

DOWN

Part B

Exercises with 1 finger remaining in the same position and 3 moving across the fingerboard

♩ = 60/180

UP

16

DOWN

UP

17

DOWN

UP

18

DOWN

♩ = 60/180

19

20

21

♩ = 60/180

UP

22

DOWN

UP

23

DOWN

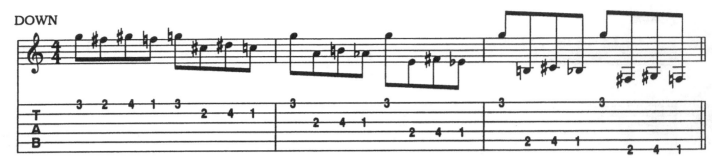

UP

24

DOWN

Part C

Exercises with 2 fingers remaining in the same position and 2 moving across the fingerboard

♩ = 60/180

Part D

Exercises with 3 fingers remaining in the same position and 1 moving across the fingerboard

♩ = 60/180

UP

40

DOWN

UP

41

DOWN

UP

42

DOWN

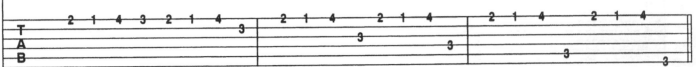

Part A

Variations of the exercises contained in Section 1

19

21

$\downarrow = 60/180$

Part A

Exercises alternating direction, with all 4 fingers
moving across the fingerboard

♩ = 60/180

Part B

Exercises alternating direction, with 1 finger remaining in the same position and 3 moving across the fingerboard

♩ = 60/180

Part C

Exercises alternating direction, with 2 fingers remaining in the same position and 2 moving across the fingerboard

♩ = **60/180**

♩ = 60/180

UP

70

DOWN

UP

71

DOWN

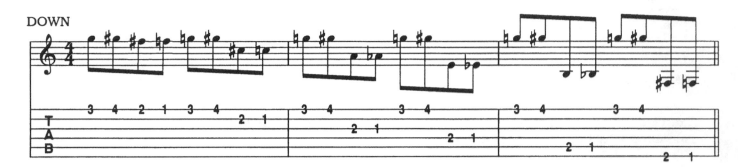

UP

72

DOWN

Part D

Exercises alternating direction, with 3 fingers remaining in the same position and 1 moving across the fingerboard

Variations of the exercises contained in Section 3

♩ = 60/180

♩ = 60/180

$\downarrow$ = 60/180

UP

86

DOWN

UP

87

DOWN

UP

88

DOWN

32

Part A

Exercises for skipping frets, with all 4 fingers moving across the fingerboard

Part B

*Exercises alternating direction, with 1 finger remaining in the same
position and 3 moving across the fingerboard*

♩ = 60/180

Part C

Exercises for skipping frets, with 2 fingers remaining in the same position and 2 moving across the fingerboard

♩ = 60/180

♩ = 60/180

Part D

*Exercises for skipping frets, with 3 fingers remaining in the
same position and 1 moving across the fingerboard*

Part A

*Exercises for skipping frets, alternating direction,
with all 4 fingers moving across the fingerboard*

Part B

Exercises for skipping frets, alternating direction, with 1 finger remaining in the same position and 3 moving across the fingerboard

♩ = 60/180

Part C

Exercises for skipping frets, alternating direction, with 2 fingers
remaining in the same position and 2 moving across the fingerboard

♩ = 60/180

♩ = 60/180

UP

114

DOWN

UP

115

DOWN
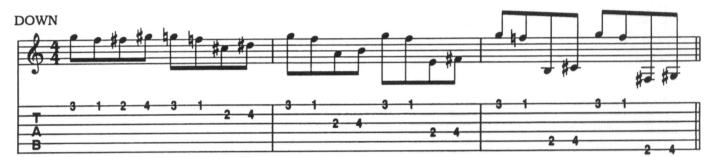

UP

116

DOWN

Part D

Exercises for skipping frets, alternating direction, with 3 fingers remaining in the same position and with 1 moving across the fingerboard

Part A

Exercises for moving between strings

♩ = 60/180

UP

124

DOWN

UP

125

DOWN

UP

126

DOWN

Part B

Exercises for skipping strings

♩ = 60/180

♩ = 60/180

UP

130

DOWN

UP

131

DOWN

UP

132

DOWN

♩ = 60/180

UP

133

DOWN

UP

134

DOWN

UP

135

DOWN

$\downarrow$ = 60/180

UP

136

DOWN

Part A

Exercises for moving back and forth between strings

Part B

Exercises for moving back and forth between strings, alternating direction

♩ = 60/180

Part C

Exercises for skipping back and forth between strings

 = 60/180

♩ = 60/180

Part D

Exercises for skipping back and forth between strings alternating direction

Part A

*Finger independence exercises centered
around finger #1 (upward motion)*

♩ = 60/180

♩ = 60/180

157

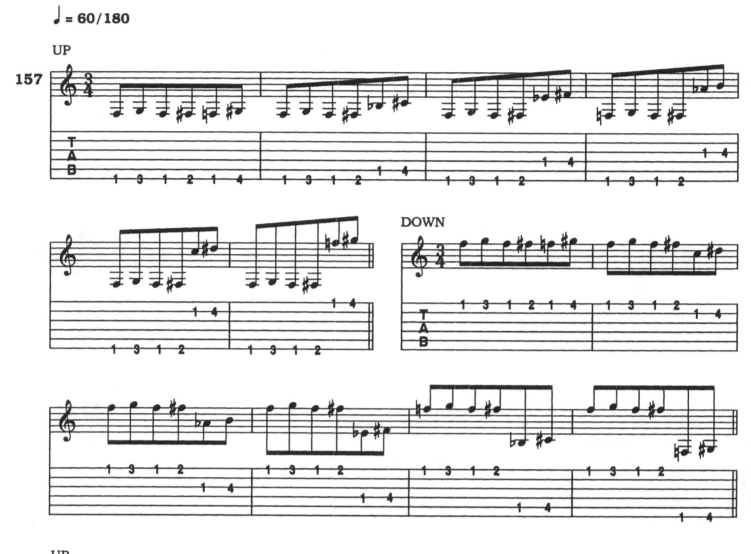

158

Part B

Finger independence exercises centered
around finger #1 (downward motion)

Part A

Finger independence exercises centered around finger #4 (upward motion)

♩ = 60/180

♩ = 60/180

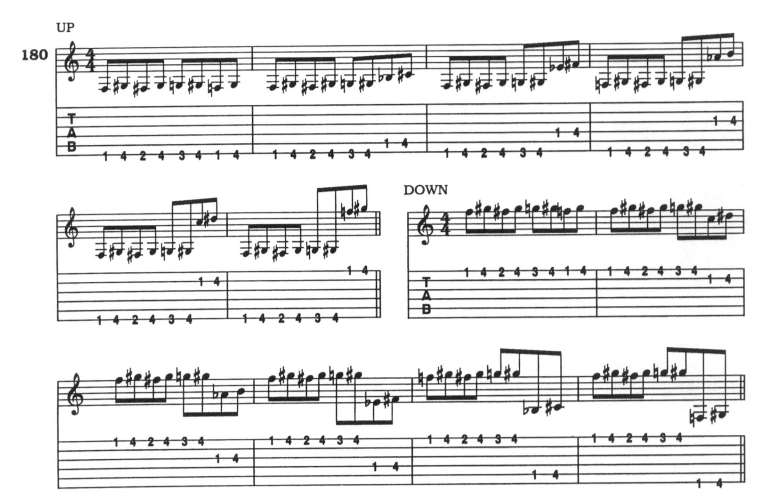

♩ = 60/180

UP

181

DOWN

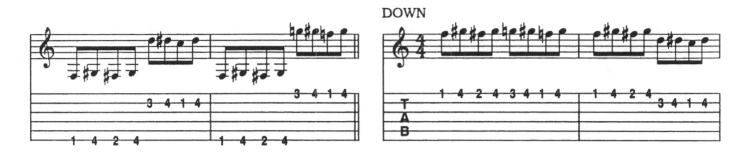

UP

182

DOWN

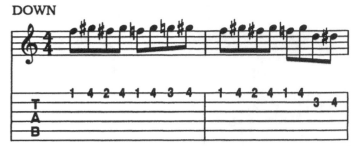

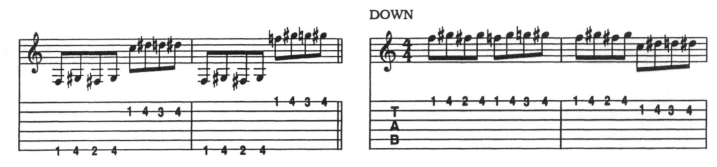

♩ = 60/180

♩ = 60/180

Part B

Finger independence exercises centered around finger #4 (downward motion)

♩ = 60/180

UP

191

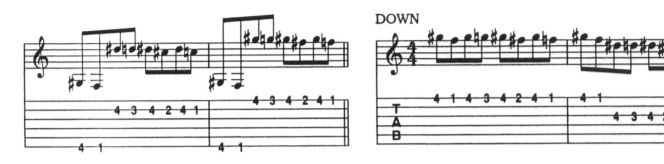

UP

192

♩ = 60/180

193

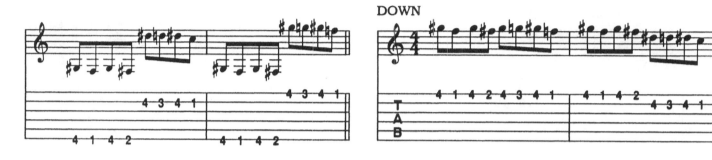

194

♩ = 60/180

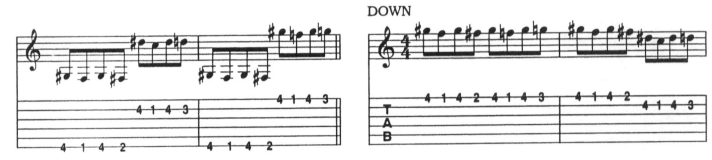

♩ = 60/180

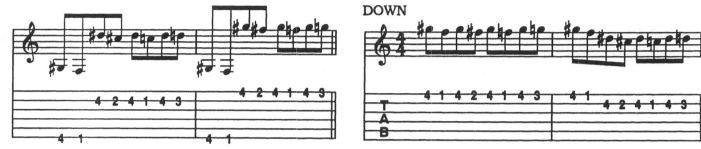

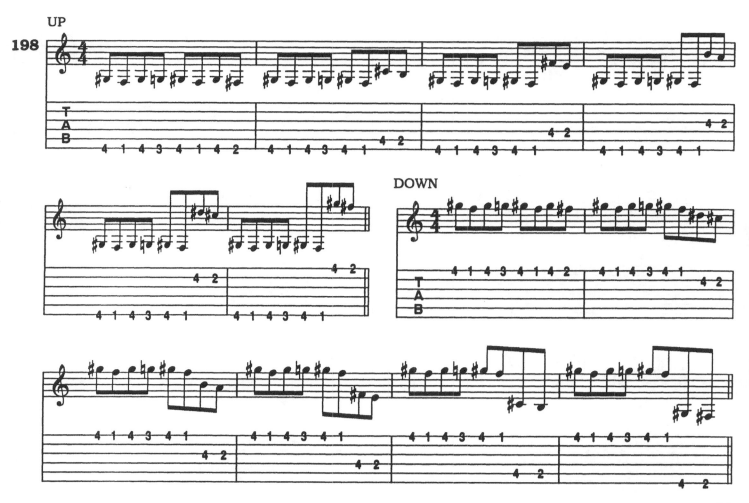

$\downarrow = 60/180$

199

200